Fouad Masri's
IS THE INJEEL CORRUPTED?
A Reply, Refutation and Rebuttal

FOUAD MASRI'S

IS THE INJEEL CORRUPTED?

A REPLY, REFUTATION AND REBUTTAL

BY

IBRAHIM BAYRAKTAR

TIME 🏛 BOOKS

Fouad Masri's
IS THE INJEEL CORRUPTED?
A Reply, Refutation and Rebuttal

ISBN (13) (Paperback): 978-1-68109-025-2
ISBN (10) (Paperback): 1-68109-025-2
ISBN (13) (Kindle): 978-1-68109-026-9
ISBN (10) (Kindle): 1-68109-026-0
ISBN (13) (ePub): 978-1-68109-027-6
ISBN (10) (ePub): 1-68109-027-9

Time Books™
an imprint of TellerBooks™
TellerBooks.com/Time_Books

 TellerBooks

www.TellerBooks.com

Manufactured in the U.S.A.

ABOUT THE IMPRINT

The *Reply, Refutation and Rebuttal* Series™ of Time Books™ publishes monographs and treatises that reply to contemporary perspectives on political, philosophical and religious issues.

Complete your collection with the following titles:

- Dinesh D'Souza's *What's So Great About America*: A Reply, Refutation and Rebuttal
- Dr. Gregory Boyd's *Myth of a Christian Nation:* A Reply, Refutation and Rebuttal
- Dr. Mel White's *What the Bible Says and Doesn't Say About Homosexuality*: A Reply, Refutation and Rebuttal
- Dr. H. M. Baagil's *Muslim-Christian Dialogue*: A Reply, Refutation and Rebuttal
- *The Communist Manifesto* of Karl Marx and Friedrich Engels: A Reply, Refutation and Rebuttal
- Fouad Masri's *Is the Injeel Corrupted?* A Reply, Refutation and Rebuttal

TIME 🏛 BOOKS

The mission of Time Books™ is to reintroduce time-tested values and truths to modern debates on political, economic, and moral issues. The imprint focuses on books and monographs dealing with society, ethics, and public policy.

THE IMPRINT

CONTENTS

CHAPTER 1. INTRODUCTION

In *Is the Injeel Corrupted?* (Crescent Project, 2006; Book Villages, 2012), Fouad Masri searches for the truth about the New Testament by tackling the question of whether the present-day Injeel (the Gospel) can be trusted, and whether Muslims should read and follow its teachings. Masri further examines the claim that the Bible is both corrupted and unreliable as a source of theological truth about Allah, His will, and the Prophets.

Relying on quotes from the Qur'an, the Bible, and history, Masri concludes that the Bible is true, reliable, and free from corruption. The error thus lies not in the Christian scriptures themselves, but in the Muslim view that the Bible is corrupted.

Masri's argumentation is flawed, however, in that it is based on superficial reasoning that only scratches the surface of Islamic theology on the question of the authenticity of the Christian scriptures. He reaches his conclusions by distorting the meaning of Islamic scripture and calling on readers' emotions to draw them towards a Christian worldview, with arguments that do not hold up to the scrutiny of tight logic. While the book successfully draws readers to sympathize with Christian thought and theology, it ultimately fails to address Muslim concerns from an intellectual perspective.

CHAPTER 2. MR. MASRI IGNORES THE FACT THAT MUSLIMS BELIEVE THE BIBLE HAS BEEN CORRUPTED

Although Mr. Masri acknowledges that Muslims believe the Bible has been corrupted, he completely misses this fact throughout his analysis. As will be seen below, he states things like "Muslims Must Read and Believe in the Injeel" (p. 12) because the Qur'an says that Muslims believe in the Qur'an given to Jesus (PbuH). However, if he had recognized that Muslims believe that this revelation has later been corrupted, he would not concluded that that Muslims should read in the Bible as it exists in its current form. Rather, he would understand that the Qur'an is referring to the message originally revealed to Moses (PbuH) and to Jesus (PbuH), which is the same message revealed to Mohammed and preserved in the Qur'an.

Mr. Masri never addresses the key concerns as to biblical corruption that cause Muslims to reject the Bible, namely:

I. ADDITIONS TO THE BIBLE

The Holy spirit was never stated in the Bible, and the verse establishing the Holy Spirit was added later in some Bibles.

II. EXCERPTS WRITTEN BY MAN

There are some parts of the Bible that were removed and later added by men. For example, the entire ending of Mark was written by a council of bishops and added to Mark as late as …

III. CHANGES IN THE OLD TESTAMENT

That the Old Testament was changed and no longer reflects the original Word of Allah (God) is made evident in its numerous contradictions. For example:
- 7,000 horsemen vs. 700 horsemen.
- Etc.

Anyone who believes that Allah is truthful and does not err should recognize that Allah could not state that both 7,000 and 700 horsemen were slayed. Therefore, this statement can only be attributed to man, who changed Allah's Word in not on this, but in many other passages as well.

IV. SELF-JUSTIFYING PROOFS

Mr. Masri points to excerpts of the Bible that purportedly prove its authenticity. For example, he cites the Book of Revelation 22:18-19: "I testify to everyone who hears the words of the prophecy of this book: if anyone adds to the, God shall add to him the plagues which are written in this book; and if anyone takes away from the words of the book of this prophecy, God shall take away his part from the tree of life and from the holy city, which are written in this book" (p. 36).

Again, Mr. Masri ignores here that Muslims believe that the Christian Scriptures, including the Book of Revelation, have been corrupted, and therefore cannot serve as evidence to Muslim that the Christian Scriptures are true, unaltered, and authentic to their original form.

CHAPTER 3. MISTRANSLATIONS, STYLISTIC PROBLEMS, CONTRADICTIONS

I. MR. MASRI'S MISTRANSLATIONS

The first major problem with this work is in translation. The book is titled "Is the Injeel Corrupted"? "Injeel" is Arabic for Gospel—the first four books of the New Testament. However, the subtitle refers to the broader New Testament ("My Search for The Truth about the New Testament") and the book itself discusses not only the New Testament, but the Old Testament as well, with a focus on the Torah and Psalms. Therefore, this book is not about whether the Gospels are corrupted, but whether the Bible in its entirety is corrupted. The book should more accurately be titled "Is the Bible Corrupted?" or "Is the Kitab al Muqaddas lil-Mesihiyeen Corrupted?," if the author wishes to mix Arabic and English, as he does throughout the book.

Mr. Masri's translation problem is not limited to the Bible; it extends to books within the Hebrew/Christian Scriptures as well. For example, in referring to the prophecies of Jesus on page 34, he makes reference to the books of Isaiah and Micah. Drawing on these books, he then states that the "Tawrat" is clear tha thte

Messiah would come to lead people to God. However, Isaiah and Micah do not form part of the Tawrat, which in English is Torah, the first five books of the Hebrew Scriptures. Rather, Isaiah and Micah form part of the Tanach, which includes not only the Torah, but all of the other Hebrew Scriptures, which together form the Christian Old Testament.

II. MR. MASRI'S STYLISTIC PROBLEMS

This brings us to our next point: the interspersing of occasional Arabic throughout the book is confusing and distracting and adds nothing of value to the book.

This book is evidently written for English-speakers. Otherwise, it would not be written in English. I am therefore confused at why the author calls certain words by their Arabic translation. For example, rather than call the Torah "Al-Tawrat" on p. 9, why doesn't the author call it "The Torah"? Isn't the English-speaking reader going to know what the Torah is? I would imagine that any intelligent reader, whether Christian or Muslim, is going to know the meaning of the words "Gospel," "Jesus," "Torah," "Moses," and "Psalms" such that using the Arabic equivalents is not necessary.

One may argue here that some Muslim readers may only recognize these words by their Arabic counterparts. For example, if the author writes "the Holy Qur'an," the reader may get confused and not realize that he means the holy book of Islam. Therefore, he provides the Arabic translation, "Al-Qur'an Al-Karim," to anticipate and prevent confusion.

Such an explanation is downright silly. If a Muslim does not know the English version to the most important words of the

Arabic language, such as "Holy Qur'an," or "Bible," then what is he doing reading a religious book in English to begin with? Reading a book in English pre-supposes that the reader have a basic knowledge of the English language, and such a basic knowledge would dictate that the reader would know the most important words of his faith in the English language. If he didn't, he wouldn't be able to understand any of the book at all!

So if this book is to be written in English, then it should be written in English. If it is to be written for Arab Muslims without knowledge of English, then it should be written in Arabic. But an English book with translations of the fundamental words of the faith into Arabic is distracting and adds no value to the book.

III. SELF-CONTRADICTIONS

Mr. Masri's text is riddled with self-contradictions. For example, in the box on page 29, he states that Jesus' message was aimed at "worshipers of one God." However, this is later changed at the bottom of the same page, which states that Jesus' message was "for all people, regardless of nationality, race, or language" (p. 29).

CHAPTER 4. MISINTERPRETATIONS AND FALSE STATEMENTS REGARDING ISLAM

I. FALSE STATEMENTS REGARDING ISLAM'S VIEWS TOWARDS THE BIBLE

The author states that "the Injeel is required for Muslims to read and believe in" (p. 8). This is false. Islam maintains that Christians have corrupted the Injeel and that in its current form, it contains all kinds of heresies, such as the idea that Jesus (PbuH) is the "son of God" and "God Himself." Therefore, they are taught to read the Qur'an only for it alone teaches that Allah and one and Jesus (PbuH), like Abraham (PbuH), Jacob (PbuH) and Moses (PbuH), was a prophet.

The author further states, "Imams commonly teach that the Injeel is one of the four holy books Muslims are required to believe in, follow, and obey" (p. 9). The author himself provides evidence showing the fallacy of the statement he just uttered by asking, "If that is true, why is the Injeel not available in religious bookstores of many Muslim countries?" (p. 9). The answer is simple; Muslims are *not* required to believe, follow, and obey the Injeel as it exists today because they believe its original form has been corrupted.

Moreover, he states that "[w]hen famous Muslim debaters claim that a version of the Bible means another version of the story, they are only exposing their ignorance of the English language," because "version" actually means "translation" (p. 44). This statement is patently false and demonstrates Mr. Masri's ignorance of Muslim views of the Bible. When Muslim debaters discuss different "versions" of the Bible, they are actually referring to different Bibles used by the different branches of Christianity. For example, Orthodox Christians, Catholics and Anglicans have many books in their Bibles that the Protestants do not, such as Tobias, Judith and 1 and 2 Maccabees. The Orthodox have the book Odes, which the Catholics, Anglicans and Protestants do not have. The Catholics, have Ecclesiasticus, called The Wisdom of Sirach by the Orthodox and Jesus the Son of Sirach by the Anglicans, which the Protestants do not have. The Anglicans have books such as Of Bel and the Dragon and The Prayer of Manasses, which the other branches of Christianity do not have. The Muslim is always left wondering: which of these Bibles are Christians supposed to believe is the true one?

II. MISINTERPRETATIONS OF THE QUR'AN

The author quotes Ayah 2:136, which states, "We believe in God and (in) that which has been revealed to us, and (in) that which was revealed to Abraham (PbuH), and Ishmael (PbuH) and Isaac (PbuH) and Jacob (PbuH) and the tribes, and (in) that which was given to Moses (PbuH) and Jesus (PbuH), and (in) that which was given to the prophets from their Lord, we do not make any distinction between any of them and to Him do we submit" to support the proposition that "Muslims Must read and Believe in the Injeel" (p. 12).

Mr. Masri fails to distinguish between believing in the revelation given to the prophets and the message contained in the Bible in its present form. Muslims believe that the Bible in its present form is corrupted. Therefore, one cannot take the fact that Muslims are to believe in the message given to Moses (PbuH) and Jesus (PbuH) as meaning that Muslims should read the Bible. Rather, it means that Muslims should believe in the messages of Moses (PbuH) and Jesus (PbuH), which were preserved in the Qur'an and changed in the Bible. Muslims should not read the Bible as it distorts the truths given to the prophets of Allah (see section above giving examples of biblical corruption).

The author similarly uses the Ayah 57:27 ("Then We made Out messengers to follow in their footsteps,. and We made Jesus son of Mary to follow, and We gave him the Gospel. And We put. compassion and mercy in the hearts of those who followed him") to support the proposition that Muslims must read and believe in the Bible. Again, the fact that Allah gave Jesus (PbuH) the Gospel does not mean that the Gospel we have today is true to the original message given to Jesus (PbuH).

Further misinterpretations of the Qur'an are made evident. Fouad Masri interprets Ayah 2:148 ("For Allah hath power over all things") to mean that "God Keeps His Word." But one does not mean the other. God can be omnipotent and yet still change His Word.

III. CHERRY PICKING FROM THE QUR'AN

Mr. Masri's further error is to cherry pick from the Qur'an. He picks only those verses that he can twist to argue that the Qur'an shows favor upon the Bible, when in reality the Qur'an condemns the Bible and the lies contained therein as a result of its corruption by the Christians and the Jews. Here are a few verses he conveniently ignores:

- Jesus (PbuH) was not the son of Allah: "Now surely it is of their own lie that they say: Allah has begotten. And truly they are liars" (Ayah 37:151-52).
- Jesus (PbuH) is not begotten of Allah: "Say: He, Allah, is One. 2. Allah is He on Whom all depend. 3. He begets not, nor is He begotten; 4. And none is like Him" (Ayah 112:1-4).
- Allah's curse is on those who say Jesus (PbuH) is the son of Allah: "And the Jews say: Ezra is the son of Allah; and the Christians say The Messiah is the son of Allah. These are the words of their mouths. They imitate the saying of those who disbelieved before. Allah's curse be on them! How they are turned away!" (Ayah 9:30).
- Jesus (PbuH) is not to be worshipped: "And behold! Allah will say: "O Jesus the son of Mary! Didst say unto men, 'Worship me and my mother as gods in derogation of Allah'?" He will say: "Glory to Thee! Never could I say what I had no right (to say)" (Ayah 5:119).
- Christians and Jews wish to put out the light of Allah: "They [Christians and Jews] desire to put out the light of Allah with their mouths, and Allah will allow nothing save the perfection of His light, though the disbelievers are averse" (Ayah 9:32).
- Jesus (PbuH) was a prophet, not Allah; the Trinity is a false doctrine: "O People of the Book! Commit no excesses in your religion: Nor say of Allah aught but the truth. Christ Jesus the son of Mary was [no more than] a messenger of Allah, and His Word, which He bestowed on Mary, and a spirit proceeding from Him: so believe in Allah and His messengers. Say not "Trinity" : desist: it will be better for you: for Allah is one Allah: Glory be to Him: [far exalted is He] above having a son. To Him belong all things in the heavens and on earth" (Ayah 4:171-172).

Mr. Fouad Masri further makes the claim that "many imams are teaching what is contrary to the Qur'anic verses above" (p. 13), namely, that the Gospel and Torah have been corrupted. Once again, he recklessly disregards the Qur'an's message: the doctrines contained in the Bible in its current forms (Jesus is the Son of Allah, Jesus is Allah, etc.) are corruptions of the original message given to the prophets (that Jesus is a prophet—not Allah). We find here evidence of Mr. Fouad Masri's intellectual dishonesty or otherwise reckless disregard of the Qur'an's message.

CHAPTER 5. ATTEMPT TO USE THE BIBLE TO SHOW THAT THE BIBLE IS TRUE

Mr. Masri then tries to use biblical verses to support the proposition that the Bible is true. Once again, his efforts are futile and he misinterprets the verses he is using.

For example, he quotes Rev 22:18-19, "If anyone adds to these things, God will add to him the plagues that are written in this book; and if anyone takes away from the words of the book of this prophecy, God shall take away his part from the Book of Life, from the holy city, and from the things which are written in this book" (p. 17). However, this quote supports the fact that God's scripture can be corrupted by man. If it were not possible, then this verse would not be necessary. Why would God pronounce the punishment for omitting from or adding to His Word if it were not possible to do to begin with?

This verse directly supports the claim that because the editors of some versions of the Bible, including the New King James Version, inserted the idea of the Trinity in 1 John 5:7 by adding a reference to the Father, Son, and Holy Ghost (this corruption did not enter many other versions, including the American Standard

Version and International Standard Version), they will not go unpunished by Allah.

Fouad Masri further uses 2Ti 3:16-17 ("All Scripture is given by inspiration of God, and is profitable for doctrine, for reproof, for correction, for instruction in righteousness, that the man of God may be complete, thoroughly equipped for every good work") to argue that God inspired all Scripture (p. 15). Yet while it is true that Allah inspired all Scripture, he did not inspire men's additions and modifications to the Scriptures.

Mr. Masri further quotes Psalm 119:89: "Your word, O Lord, is eternal; it stands firm in the heavens." It should be noted that although Allah's Word is eternal, man is capable of corrupting the revelation of Allah's Word put in human form. It is possible for anyone to publish a Bible with all kinds of additions and omissions. However, Allah has responded to these deceivers throughout history by raising up new prophets to restore Allah's Word and His message to humanity.

CHAPTER 6. MUSLIM REPLIES TO MR. MASRI'S ARGUMENTS

I. ARE HUMANS STRONGER THAN GOD?

Fouad Masri goes on to argue, "If God's word was revealed to humans, and humans corrupted God's word, doesn't that make humans stronger than God? Impossible!" (p. 20). Similarly, he implies the Muslim argument that man corrupted God's word to be irrational: "God is stronger than any human, and while humans may try to concel God's word, His truth still stands out clearly from error" (p. 31-32).

Mr. Masri is right here, and the revelation of the Qur'an proves it. Although man corrupted Allah's Word, Allah continued to raise up prophets to restore His Word, which was finally sealed with the last prophet, Muhammad (PbuH). God was victorious in the end.

II. "WHY WOULD GOD ALLOW CHRISTIANS TO LIVE IN IGNORANCE?"

Mr. Masri asks, "If the Injeel was changed, why would God allow early Christians to live in ignorance of God's will for nearly six hundred years (the time between the Injeel's supposed corruption and the coming of the prophet of Islam?)" (p. 25). This question on one hand is problematic because it assumes that the Christian scriptures were immediately corrupted. However, this was not the case. Allah's message was preserved by many of the Christians in the early years of Christianity. Though there were some that wished to worship Jesus as God, these did not win institutional recognition until the church councils of the fourth century and thereafter began to label as heretics those who viewed Jesus as a mere man, teacher and prophet. Corruption of the church did not take place institutionally until the First Council of Nicaea in 325, and the corruption of the Bible did not occur until later, in the local Council of Carthage of 397, which listed the books in the modern day Bible. This list, which includes several heretical gospels and excludes others, was not accepted on an ecumenical basis until the Second Council of Nicaea in 787, which adopted the canon of the Bible of the Council of Carthage. Therefore, the corruption of the Church took place slowly and over centuries, and many of the Christians of the first five centuries of Christianity did not submit to the worship of Jesus and other heretical practices of the Church. These would later become Muslim converts to Allah's true, unadulterated religion, as Islam spread from Arabia to the Levant, northern Africa, and ultimately Europe.

III. WHEN DID BIBLICAL CORRUPTION TAKE PLACE?

The author states that "Since the Prophet Muhammad commanded all Muslims to read the Injeel, it must have been corrupted after his death. He wouldn't have instructed us to believe and read a corrupted book, would he?" (p. 26). Mr. Masri falsely attributes instructions to Prophet Muhammad (PbuH), who never instructed his followers to read or believe in the Bible. The Qur'an clearly teaches that the beliefs of the Christians are corrupt and profane: "the Christians say The Messiah is the son of Allah. These are the words of their mouths. They imitate the saying of those who disbelieved before. Allah's curse be on them!" (9:30). Yet rather than read and heed the words of the Qur'an, Fouad Masri distorts them. On page 12, for example, he takes Sura 2:136 ("We believe in God and (in) that which has been revealed to us, and (in) that which was revealed to Abraham, and Ishmael and Isaac and Jacob and the tribes, and (in) that which was given to Moses and Jesus") and twists them to mean that Muslims must "read and believe in the Injeel" (p. 12), even though the verse states no such thing. It states that Jesus received a revelation, not that the book that Christians believe in today is that revelation.

IV. "NO OPPORTUNITY FOR CORRUPTING THE BIBLE IN THE EYEWITNESS STAGE"

Mr. Masri writes, "In the Eyewitness Stage there was no opportunity for corrupting the Bible, since the eyewitnesses were alive. Those who were alive and knew the truth-whether believers or not-would protest any changes to the story" (p. 37). Yet just because the eyewitnesses protest alternate accounts does not make these alternate accounts disappear. Most people at the birth of Christianity did not believe that Jesus Christ rose from the dead, despite the testimony of the Gospels. Most people, including the reigning Roman government, did not agree with the accounts of the resurrection, which explains why early Christians remained a persecuted minority group.

CHAPTER 7. A BRIEF HISTORY OF THE CORRUPTION OF THE BIBLE

I. UNINTENTIONAL AND INTENTIONAL CORRUPTION

The author expresses his conundrum as to how Muslims can explain that the Bible was corrupted: "As a mu'min (believer in God), I could not reconcile how God's word could be changed by mere humans" (p. 18). The explanation is however neither difficult or incredible, and can be divided into unintentional and intentional corruptions.

1. Unintentional Corruption

Fouad Masri asks the reader: "Who is the person that centered his or her efforts on changing a message sent from God? What evil person would corrupt the Injeel, betraying God and the Christians?" (p. 24).

It is first important to point out here that Muslims do not necessarily believe that some "evil person" corrupted the Injeel. While it is true that some evil persons were involved, much of the corruption was due to error, mistranslation and loss of original manuscripts. The process took place over hundreds of years, and resulted in a Bible that today teaches a message very much different from that preserved in the Qur'an.

a. Loss of Original Texts and Manuscripts

Similarly, though Jesus did not die on the cross ("they killed him not, nor did they cause his death on the cross" (Ayah 4:157)), Christians added to the Gospels to make it appear as such. It is widely acknowledged by scholars that the ending of the Gospel of Mark (16:9-20) has been lost in all of the earliest manuscripts and the current ending is a later addition by the church.

Christian apologists may argue that this addition changes nothing substantial in the Gospel, since both the crucifixion and resurrection are discussed earlier (in Mark 15:22-38, and Mark 16:2-8, respectively) and Mark 16:9-20 only discusses Jesus' appearance to Mary Magdalene, to two walking into the country, and to the eleven disciples, all of which is discussed in the other three Gospels.

However, although Mark 16:9-20 doesn't change anything substantial, it shows that Christians change their scriptures. Whether or not the leaders who created the ending is immaterial; the fact that leaders can alter or add to the scriptures shows us that the Bible should not be trusted as the authentic Word of Allah. For every instance in which the church admits to changing a part of scripture, how many other instances are there in which the change was hidden and concealed in order to deceive readers?

b. Scribal Error

Scribal error can most likely explain the many self-contradictions recorded in the Old Testament, since these errors do not in any way change any doctrines as intentional modifications would seek to do. Examples of scribal errors leading to self-contradictions include:

- Seven hundred horsemen in 2 Samuel 8:4 ("David took from him one thousand chariots, **seven hundred horsemen**, and twenty thousand foot soldiers") versus seven thousand horsemen in 1 Chronicles 18:4 (David took from him one thousand chariots, **seven thousand horsemen**, and twenty thousand foot soldiers).
- Seven hundred charioteers in 2 Samuel 10:18 ("Then the Syrians fled before Israel; and David killed **seven hundred charioteers** and forty thousand horsemen of the Syrians") versus seven thousand charioteers in 1 Chronicles 19:18 ("Then the Syrians fled before Israel; and David killed **seven thousand charioteers** and forty thousand foot soldiers of the Syrians").

c. Mistranslation

Finally, because there is no one official version of the Bible or preservation of any original text in an original language (as there is with the one Arabic Qur'an, preserved in its original form), there are countless problems that arise as a result of translations. As a result, once has thousands of different versions of the Bible, with dozens or hundreds of disparate translations within the same language, and sometimes various editions of the same translation within the same language. All of these different versions have differences as to nuance and translations. Christians and Jews are unable to point to one authoritative text, as do Muslims. Even the earliest extant manuscripts are copies of original texts and often contain scribal errors or contradictions among themselves. These differences are not due to intentional human interference, but rather to human error and the limitations of language.

2. Intentional Corruption

Intentional corruption results from man's desire to impose his will on Allah and deceive others into following him. This occurred in the early church and in the years preceding the rise of Prophet Muhammad (PbuH). One example of this is the insertion of the doctrine of the Trinity in 1 John 5:7, which undermines Allah's message of His oneness.

Allah has taught all of the prophets the same message: God is one and man is to worship no other gods. Yet Jews and Christians have insisted on inventing and worshipping other gods throughout history. In Exodus, we read of the Jews creating and offering sacrifices to a golden calf when Moses (PbuH) was delayed in coming down from the mountain. Aaron said to them, "This is your god, O Israel, that brought you out of the land of Egypt!" (Exo 32:4). In 1 Kings, we read that among the Israelites, there were only 7,000 that did not bow down in worship to the god Baal (1Ki 19:18).

Christians are guilty of the same sin. Despite Jesus's message that Allah is one, Christians invented the doctrine of the Trinity, asserting that God, His son Jesus, and the Holy Spirit are each individually God and together form one God. To support this teaching, verses were added to certain versions of the Bible. For example, the King James Version adds to 1 John 5:7 "the Father, the Word, and the Holy Ghost: and these three are one," words which were not included in the vast majority of the earliest extant manuscripts of the Bible, and which are not included in many other versions, including the American Standard Version and International Standard Version. Certain Christians added this clause to support the idea that Allah is comprised of a trinity and to thus justify polytheistic worship.

3. Allah's Responsibility to Protect His Word

The author further seems to think it is Allah's responsibility to keep sinful humans from corruption His Word: "If God revealed the Injeel, I reasoned, wasn't it His responsibility to keep it from corruption?" (p. 18). It is not Allah's responsibility to keep man from corrupting His Word or to prevent man from sinning in any other way. When Allah created man, he allowed man to freely transgress Allah's commandments. This was part of Allah's plan to create man with free will and to mete out punishment and reward on Judgment Day.

II. HOW THE BIBLE WAS CORRUPTED

The early church was comprised of disciples of Jesus (PbuH) who believed His message that Allah was one and that Jesus (PbuH) was His prophet. However, within the first three centuries of Christianity, a group of bishops began teaching that Jesus (PbuH) was fully God and not created. A second group of bishops known as the Arians resisted this false teaching and held to Jesus' original message. They split off from the church at the First Council of Nicaea in 325. To this day, the Arians continue to teach that Jesus was a created man, and are thus much closer to Islam than the Nicaea Christians that split from them.

The error of the Church in equating Jesus (PbuH) with Allah led to repeated controversies and church splits. In 680, for example, the Third Council of Constantinople rejected Monothelitism and held that Jesus (PbuH) had both a human will and a divine will. The Monothelites, who held that Jesus (PbuH) had only one will, split off from the rest of the Church.

Allah rose up Prophet Muhammad to restore the original message of Jesus (PbuH), which is the same message of Abraham

(PbuH), Moses (PbuH) and the other prophets: Allah is one and no object is to be worshipped beside him. Although Allah originally raised up these prophets to lead man away from polytheistic worship of objects and false gods, after the rise of Christianity, men began to worship other men. Jesus (PbuH) and Mary became objects of man's worship. Rather than direct worship towards Allah, man prayed to and worshipped Jesus (PbuH) and Mary.

Statues of Jesus (PbuH), his mother Mary, and Christian saints were erected in churches and Christians

Allah raised up Prophet Muhammad (PbuH) to restore Allah's original message and the message given to Jesus (PbuH), who said "Never could I say what I had no right (to say). Had I said ['Worship me and my mother as gods'], Thou wouldst indeed have known it. Thou knowest what is in my heart, though I know not what is in Thine" (5:119-121). Prophet Muhammad was Allah's final prophet and seal to eternally restore Islam as Allah's true religion through the Qur'an, the "Invincible Book" (41:41): "Falsehood cannot come at it from before or behind it: a revelation from the Wise, the Praised One" (41:42).

CHAPTER 8. CONCLUSION

I. SOME STRONG POINTS IN THE BOOK

It would be disingenuous to point out only the flaws in Mr. Masri's book without pointing out the strengths, a few of which are found therein. Mr. Masri points out that:

- "We do not have the original, physical copy of Al-Qur'an Al-Karim" (p. 35);
- "We also do not have the original, physical copy of the Tawrat, Zabur, or Injeel today" (p. 35).

II. CONCLUDING THOUGHTS

In concluding, I wish to answer the questions asked by Mr. Masri on page 48:

- When was the Injeel corrupted? Over thousands of years.
- Who would do such a thing? Jews, the Church and scribes.
- What motivation would someone have to change the Injeel? Much of this was motivated by Jews and Gentiles to believe that they were God's chosen people, first through God's covenant with Abraham, which Jews believe passed to Isaac, and then through God's supposed covenant with man through Jesus (PbuH), which Christians believe opened the covenant to all who believe. The Christian Scriptures in their current form justify God's favor towards

the Jews, his genocide and destruction of other peoples (Jericho, Heshbon, Bashan, Amalek, Midianites, Hivites, Philistines, etc.), all of which teach that Allah is a cruel, vengeful god who instructs the destruction of entire peoples, including innocent women and children, and which today many Jews use to justify their destruction of the Palestinian people and the taking of their land.

Although man corrupted God's Word, in the end, God prevailed by raising up Prophet Mohammed (PbuH) and restoring His word through the Holy Qur'an.

9 781681 090252